Nocturnal House

Mike Greenacre

Nocturnal House

For Tracy, Jonathan, Jaime & Chris
and my parents and family

Nocturnal House
ISBN 978 1 76109 018 9
Copyright © text Mike Greenacre 2020
Cover image: Angie A. Phillips

First published 2020 by
Ginninderra Press
PO Box 3461 Port Adelaide 5015 Australia
www.ginninderrapress.com.au

Contents

Nocturnal House
  Nocturnal House   11
  Poets Fishing   12
  A Gathering of Words   13
  On Writing   15
  A Hitchhiker's Guide to Poetry   16
  Fremantle Arts Centre   17
  Novelist & Poet Over a Beer   19
  Rewriting You   21
  Scuff Marks   22
  'Voicebox' Fremantle   24
  The Poem Itself   26

From Bar to Spyglass
  From Bar to Spyglass   29
  Supermoon   30
  Moon on Monday   31
  Necklace of Words   32
  Poetry Downpour   34
  Chasing a Poem   35
  Ronsardian Ode to Poets   36
  Nature's Page   37
  Vagabonds   38
  Haiku   39
  Senryu   42
  Tanka   43
  Australian Gallery   44
  Keyhole   46

Swan River Reflections
  Swan River Reflections   49

Collecting Days	51
Water Polo Boy	53
As If Helping	54
The Old Bakery	56
Time Tunnel	58
Snapshots to Now	60
Where I'm From	62
The Caning	63
Fast Food Wrappers	64
Sacred Places	66
Trapped in Language	67
Back-seat Vision	68
Passengers	69
Man in the Boat	70
FA Cup Nights	71
Strumming Up the Past	73
Neighbourhood	75

The Shape of Love

The Shape of Love	79
The Real You	82
A Last Song	83
Deceased	85
Rasa	86
So Many Words	87
Penguin Boys	89
Knitting Bones	92
12-bar Bones	94
Skeleton	95
Closing Time	97
Third Generation	100
Changing Speed	102

Missing Pieces	104
The Wave	107
Parents and Poems	108
Applecross Jetty Bed	109

Recipe of Love

Recipe of Love	113
Gone	115
Eros	116
argument of seduction	117
Love That Can't be Tamed	118
Symmetry	119
AFL Dogs Grand Final	120
The Gift of Love	121
Doorways of Love	122
Dark Side of the Moons	123
Love From Scott's View	125
Where I Found Love	127
Love Into Words	128
From the Cottesloe Hotel	129
Love in Lockdown	130
The Music of Love	131
The Last to Go	132

Rottnest Ghost

Rottnest Ghost	135
The Hunger Beneath	137
Surfcatting on the Swan	138
Flight of Love	140
Not to Know	143
Intruders	145
Being Frank	147
Haibun	149

Fremantle: in Spirit and Voice	150
Preston Point	152
Porongorups to Bluff Knoll	155
Windhold Day	158
Norseman Moon	161
Looking Glass	163
Raffles Hotel on Song	164
Snake Pit Scarborough Beach	166
Petrarchan Ode to Woodstock	168
To the Edge of Now	169
Regret	171
Dispiriting	172
Stumps	173
Acknowledgements	174
Thanks	175

Nocturnal House

Nocturnal House

I sit naked
on the kitchen chair
the fridge
murmuring through me

mesh lightshade creating
a lattice field
that catches my stare

climbing, swinging carelessly

until after moonlight
minds pause and walls stand
as worded guardians
over the incomplete

a cock crows and I know
I've been too long

that daylight leaks
what the night hoards.

Poets Fishing

for John Kinsella

It was a time
I reel close towards me,
a distant glow
on the tide of mind

a meeting at the Oddfellows
Hotel, Fremantle where we
measured our distance
in jokes and full-strength lager

cast words as fine lines
searching the river's mouth,
tugged at connections
above a vast literary bed.

As victims of loss and love
we shared situations as fresh bait
to lure revelations
from out of our depths:

'I want what you already
have,' you said
and signed my copy
of your first catch.

A Gathering of Words

for Maureen Sexton

An arranged meeting –
our cyber-friendship
to be made real,
'poetry readings'
as a place   like an
interactive page.

My eyes raced
through the Perth
Cultural Market stalls,
hoping they would
stop and unlock
a returning smile.

The chirp of belonging
reached through the
shelter of Moreton Bay
fig and flame trees
bursting forth
on the heels of spring

as I watched the
faces stand naked
from crowd   their
voices pushing words
towards the Art
Gallery   while

human traffic
revolved behind
as a steady back-
beat to the squawk
and sudden flight
of images released.

Still no you, as I
imagined you to be,
our cyber words
hold us as strangers,
face to face in the
gathering of words.

On Writing

the urge
stalks you

as a hungry line

and eats up
your sleep

A Hitchhiker's Guide to Poetry

I couldn't listen for a while,
make sense of   or
understand their ravings,
from the start I
resisted your crafted
face, thinking
I didn't want to know.

Many times I
defended myself like this –
like a right not to
hear or grow, inwardly
I could search
without threat
and be sure
I wouldn't fail.

Outside makes too
many demands,
expects a certain
commitment which becomes
too self-conscious
to follow through
and pretend it's
really you.

No, the life for me
was in here
where I could
attack and withdraw
without accepting any of it.

Fremantle Arts Centre

I would sit amongst a
table full of eager minds
exploring literary forms
and imagine the dark
hysteria climbing
these gothic asylum walls.

The shadow through
barred windows at night:
a ghost's head? Our laughter
waking up the past.

I heard of the sudden
'cold spots' or 'drops in
temperature' that can creep
beneath your coats
and the woman who jumped
to her death from the first
floor who still roams the halls
looking for her child…

'And who can withstand
the current of their
environment?' Elizabeth
Jolley would break our
silence… 'You can't
shout into a book
and say stop!'

How would these cells
reply to the labels of now:
'Lecture Theatre' and
'Studio 1-20'?

Do we relish in being
part   of the asylum's
savage heart?

Novelist & Poet Over a Beer

The reason you feel
you can't just
get down and write
a poem
is that you're too hung
up about form – stanza length
style & meaning, whether
a sonnet or cinquain
should grow out, not
close you in I said.

The basic building block
of a story
is the paragraph
and anyone can write
a sentence   he
said   but the poem
is highly stylised
and clings to
images like a monkey swinging
through lattices
of meaning.

And yet the poem offers
more freedom – there is
no precise form
or rules that
tick inside like a fuse.

Some editors
say things like:
'W.B. Yeats
rewrote his poems
30 to 40 times – I feel
you stop work too
soon' while another
accepts because it's
raw & you.

It sounds like you
leave too many things
open to chance
he said, I'm more
careful –
people like you
don't exist
in my book.

Good, I said
then it must be
your buy.

Rewriting You

I wanted to tell them I'd been
away, caught another metre
and slipped between their lines:

> Good, but as verse it's hopeless –
> it's practically prose

> Your poem was certainly evocative
> but I wasn't sure of what!

Comments that shape
and suspend literary culture – squeeze
perception through a tiny hole:

> Too much statement
> and not enough poetry

> You must breathe the classics
> before you call this voice your own

Makes me grieve for poets
absorbing encouragement from
the curl of paper and words alone.

Scuff Marks

After I'd sent off my three
poems, packed together tightly
arm in arm, side stepping
like the three Amigos
doing the metaphorical dance

I ran to the bookcase
knowing 'those' two lines
flew like a bullet
from somewhere   and the
mind's editor
wouldn't let them sleep.

First thoughts were Templeman,
mentally following his words
up and down the Fremantle hill,
next Burke's flight logs of
the Kimberley scattering
landscape images wide and deep.

As time began to chisel
the words on every poet's lips,
I grabbed at Jenkins, McCauley
Lansdown, Caddy and Catlin
catching each by their first jackets
and flipping them helplessly
on their backs to see all.

It took me two years to
find out what I thought
wasn't real, so now I've
quit this game of searching
in case my scuff marks
can be seen on every kerb.

'Voicebox' Fremantle

I couldn't read tonight
just something
inside me
wouldn't let this
urgency out.

I'd signed the list
and had my number in the queue
as if at the dole office –
feeling the nerves rise
as I fumbled for my excuse.

The place hasn't changed –
Clancy's overflowing with
local voices, some tables
curled around the stage
as arms of belonging

and the bar
looming over us with
expectation   from the side
whispering, 'Dutch courage
is better than none!'

Like a determined toddler
the poem could stand on its own
but it's me, the nervous father
who couldn't face
the chance of a fall.

Luck quickly swung
back towards me
as Jo lingered past with
the list – I grabbed it like the
Artful Dodger

and swiftly
returned it 'less full'…
saying   there's
something inside
that just won't let me in.

The Poem Itself

is where you want it
yet how you arrive
depends on where you've been

from hallways of regret or guilt
to beds of love or lust
there's this place

more like a room
that becomes too crowded
and yearns for release

from a window to an afternoon
breeze – the Fremantle Doctor,
that sudden turn of words.

A life sentence in ways
of late nights and lost sleep
leaving promises to partners

you can't always keep,
manipulator of time
from seeker to event

those urges that push you
unhinged   become
the poem itself.

From Bar to Spyglass

From Bar to Spyglass
for Dick Alderson

I don't often get this far
sip as many words
from another's glass

but tonight I'm almost
halfway through
this jug of verse

before the first speaker
mounts the stage
to break the ice of words.

And you smile back
your reflection as
the bold face of Galileo

refuting Aristotle's Laws,
ride the Copernican Theory
that leads your spyglass

further out, past the moon
and it's myth-givings
towards the limits

of science and
mathematical formula
to what remains

beyond words

Supermoon

Last June there was
a giant spotlight
that transformed night's
black coat to blue

a coincidence they say –
the new moon coincides
with its closest approach to us
four times a year, when earth

moon and sun are all in line
like snooker balls, bringing the
largest tides from a stronger
gravitational pull   earth-
quakes and volcanoes feared.

The 'moon illusion' is in
your eyes they say, and yet
the moon this night was the
largest in nearly twenty years.

Winged clouds as giant seagulls
drift with your magnetic
charm   and the stars are
shadowed by your wide smile

as Selene, the Greek Goddess
of Moon drives her chariot
with mad passion across
the heavens at full speed.

Moon on Monday

There's something about
the moon on Monday,
this time of night
when the air is as still
as a vacuum, life echoing
like an empty room.

And you out late walking
with Julie and our baby
pushing our domestic yard
down streets, leaving
an extended verbal trail,
the steady moonbeam
coaxing you on, reaching
out further than words.

The familiar neighbour's
lights stare their welcome
and cicadas count out
your steps like a coded
password, as Ben the dog
barks through the shadow
of grass trees, creating
an imaginary shield.

Yes, there's something
about the moon on Monday,
this time of night, as if
it knows I'm here alone
waxing and waning
what's within.

Necklace of Words
for Chris, on his return

He wasn't going to come
and I knew it,
would say at the last minute
that it wasn't for him

though he asked me to take him
to my favourite coffee shops
and hang-outs, as if
he didn't want to trespass
but sort of 'know' where I live

and although he nodded
to my suggestion with agreeing
hands to come along to the
writing group, knew he'd withdraw
the verbal handshake
and retreat somewhere within.

But this time I decided to
outsmart the fox at his
own game, sending him a text
not too long before the
arranged pick-up time:

'I've got you a notebook
and a pen,' to which he
lowered his head just like
a fox and gave in.

The room was full with poets
and words that only friendship
could know as we entered
and although he fitted the bill,
suddenly vanished

into himself and I thought my
big ideas had done him in,
until he read his sonnet
which shone like a jewel
in a necklace of words.

Poetry Downpour

I located the drip
above our heads
at the Moon Café
and we moved our words
along to the next chair

as if droplets were
tapping us on the shoulder
like subtle reminders
of who has the last say.

Before lightning struck
thunder roared its warning
as metaphor drowning
out the surface meaning
of words with complex
orchestrations

then rain began to
thump down on the roof
like a heavy 12-bar blues beat
swallowing frustrated voices
caught in a poetry downpour.

Chasing a Poem

Reworking old poems is like
driving your car between
two posts – the closer
you get to one idea, the
further you go from the rest.

I look at the little bits
of verse on separate sheets
across the years and
realise time can dislocate
as well as heal.

Flipping eagerly through
my file, hoping there is
one dressed near complete,
I find I have to remodel
more than save.

Maybe I need to stand back
from the edge and
throw in a line hoping
to catch a verse,
but there's too much of me
lying as dead-weight
for imagination to bear.

'I should be writing!' I call
out to the night, watching
me flit from journal
to facebook or any trail that
can turn into something else,
might lead me there.

Ronsardian Ode to Poets

I can't write freely to a given form
can't see the sense
in making thoughts fit someone else's law,
it makes me tense
to see originality die
inside a prescription that counts each sigh,
throw out caution
with each portion –
that zeal with words is your desire.

Nature's Page

A bird   a raven   silently
stalking in the tree above
at the WA Writers' Week

just crapped on my page…
no kidding, a direct hit,
something I didn't
at first think was shit.

How many times walking
have I steered my life
between these excretions
and never been grazed or
cornered by fallout?

But here I've been hit
and now I can't settle without
a cursive eye skyward, keep
moving my chair to 'dodge'
the shadow above.

From above, there is no
redemption   just a suggestion
that it's time to move on.

Some birds can pick you out
like a sniper they say,
as we search our program
and ring the writer we aim for.

Vagabonds

I don't know where
these poems
come from
but their constant
tramping
across the brow
of tomorrow
keeps me
at arm's length
from sleep.

Haiku

cicadas' steady drone
counts out afternoons
the rhythm of rising heat

barramundi
silver flashes
eluding our lines

jabirus are jets
their long legs and black beaks
disproportionate

crocodiles
their shiver-keen coat and eye
sensitive radar

fallen pine cones
browned closed fingers to the sky

seagull's wings
curl around buildings
effortlessly

plane trees
green silence
in the breeze

grey sky
down Barrack Street
seagull squawk

first up in the city
the magpie lark call

Senryu

It's just natural
for the moon to rise in you
when our words are few

outdoor poetry
sown before blown on the wind
the birds chant it now

Tanka

Magpie calls beckon
Through early-morning window
Skipping up and down
The scales with apparent ease
To bring people out to feed

Australian Gallery

Set apart   as the
distinctions of cultural
landscape   we
cannot move without
the aura and
charm of lifestyle
following us from
town to face.

Streeton's *Golden Summer* –
outback sheep and
scorching sun glaze
observes a greater
silence within,
contentment
of sheep bleating
through the wind,
the rustle of ears

to sudden crowds
and bar-room
jeers   the music of
Roberts, the more
refined with parasol
and petticoats
raising ankles and
finding another brow.

Movement of landscape –
places we all know
and interpret
swing in canvas colour
and hanging lights
to stairs – levels
we cannot escape.

A product of local lives,
of a hundred years –
artistic and philosophic
sweat that pours
through the character
of sun, surf and
outback identities
from Streeton,
Roberts, McCubbin and
Conder who led
the Heidelberg dance.

The pain and pride
of voices echo
through our distant
halls of industry
as a physical world
shaping
the mirror in us all.

Keyhole

Surgery

I was told
they need
some thin
poems to
squeeze
through
the key-
hole of
imagin-
ation
with-out
touching
the
sides.

Swan River Reflections

Swan River Reflections

Writing about old times
is like dinkying your life on the handlebars –
wanting to re-capture the thrills
and 'craft' the spills
that sent us somehow hurtling
through the spaces in memory.

Riding flat-out with 'no hands'
the river is an ancient sentinel
drawing memories from under bushes
within drunken moments of backyard shows
or from those bobbing patiently as a net
ready to sweep the river's vastness.

The echoes of well-trodden streets and houses
become voices turning me back around
to the smell of crammed cigarette-hazed bedrooms,
the lure of vying eyes and the thrust of one-liners
shooting between girls or mates
like throbbing beats of twelve-bar blues guitar.

But from this forty-odd-year distance
the control seems good, reason climbing
as a mountaineer above all cares
until the sudden fine edges of words
create a precipice, flanked by truth's nakedness
and the safety of other versions.

Writing about old times
is to dinky your life on the handlebars –
wanting to 'open up'
what time and circumstance conceal,
spilling traces of our journeys
that ride the moonlight of teenage lives.

Collecting Days

for Chris

Tonight I see your image
as a ghost on skype,
two brothers separated
by circumstance
and chance's frown.

As you open that wide smile
you swallow the years
and we are suddenly
that 'inseparable pair'

charging at life's fun
and adventure with the
fire of childhood burning
through time's tableaux
of innocence and dare.

'Do you remember our
collecting days?' you
ask   as if time
could erase those
early Sunday mornings

and long hot afternoons
that stretched the limits
of our neighbourhood
and the twilight
of childhood's range.

Matchbox tops, cigarette
packet covers, bottle tops
and beer and wine labels
to stash in tins as heirlooms
or glue in brown paper
files as emblems of our time.

'I wish I still had them'
you concede to the
past's heartstrings loosely
tying our words and lives,
pulled tightly back again.

Water Polo Boy

Casual physique
the men came with bags
to Beatty Park Aquatic Centre,
their fingers clenched
like fists of war.

Towels flung over shoulders
as a last-minute swill,
tracksuit brands
shaping the parade with
mateship cries and
clinging girlfriends.

At first I was flyweight
but could wriggle like a tadpole
through bodies and arms
and out-smart the
dirty play of old men.

Training twice a week, playing
grade games on Thursday nights
and under-age on Saturdays,
squeezing in schoolwork
as an out-grown friend.

This was my first escape,
a mental net from
nine to seventeen –
I never missed a game.

As If Helping

for Julie and Jenni

'Teacher on abuse charges'
dating back the years
to my old primary school,
a suburban man
is all the paper told.

Without name, I know
it is you – the one
who kept girls in at lunch-time
and pulled down the blinds
so we couldn't see
your mind working with
'selected' girls after school.

As boys we would laugh
and fire blank accusations
at your windows
until crazed eyes glared
from your suddenly adult
frame, telling us to go home
and forget our fantasy.

Before I rang old friends
my heart still disbelieved
what we laughed true – they
said you'd come and sit
next to them in class
as if helping, while
the rest worked around you.

Awaiting trial?
There's a generation
of silent, screwed-
up reasons
for not coming forth.

The Old Bakery

Across Canning Highway
always seemed like
an 'out of bounds' zone,
where we'd skip between
traffic as trespassers,
sneak our bikes
as 'getaway' strategies
across the road.

We came across it by chance
our childhood quest
for adventure luring down
laneways   this time
behind the highway deli
on this other side,
imagination driving
us into hidden places.

Surrounded it with our bikes
like a posse on horseback –
the handlebars of mystery
clasped tightly in our hands,
then quickly lay down
our metal stallions to
force entry through a broken
louvre above a well-oiled
key-locked door.

The old bakery, hidden away
as a childhood dream of
a meeting place of our own –
the air thick with dust motes
that twinkled as diamonds
in sunlight strangled through
slits in boards, with wood-
fired ovens from ceiling to floor.

'But what did you do there?'
my brother now asks, as if
purpose was the director of
early teenage minds
…and I remember thinking
how luck was our accomplice
that day we turned the key to a
well-oiled locked door.

Time Tunnel

for Chris

Like a magnetic force
I was lured
to your alternative
lifestyle and
artistic workings.

As children we
shared time's adventures
and wove life
patterns from our
crochet rug upbringing –
threads sequenced
in well-trained space.

How I envied you
with a younger
brother's frustration –
never seeming as good,
confident or
direction sure.

As teenagers I
couldn't understand
the way you
closed me off, as
if you had outgrown
our childhood yard.

Like a trapeze artist
you swung from
the academic tree,
locked yourself
away in files –
mathematics and science
your guardians,
your bars

and I leapt for shelter
as a frightened
voice seeking the
mateship of other lives
and vices that
didn't compete with
academic minds.

The irony of grown-up
years finds me as
teacher – game-master
on the competitive
wheel

and you as actor
who contemplates and
traces life's sinews,
manipulates
the threat of time.

Snapshots to Now

Click 1:

The Narrows Bridge Opening Ceremony,
almost before my time in 1959,
the suit and tie and long-dressed audience
sitting as patient guests to history
as the tape was cut, releasing lane-fulls
of walkers to cross to the other side as cars
that would one day take over this town.

Click 2:

The Mitchell Freeway construction
on reclaimed land 1967, I was old enough
to work the Kodak Instamatic camera
and catch the earthworks and graders
pull the northern suburbs towards us,
over and underpasses
steering a faster pace to lives.

Click 3:

The Stirling Bridge arched across our
days and evenings from 1974, another bridge
linking Perth to Freo along a major arterial road
and we sat beneath as merry sailors, around a
treasure chest of live-music acts and beverages
that sprang from the Left Bank Hotel
a handful of years further down the road.

Click 4:

These three bridges have spanned my lifetime
from ten-pound Pom passenger to now
and like a poem, firm constructions
that travel with the deftness of a fisherman's net
across the Swan River – collecting and
carrying memories in the ebb and flow
of progress with the gush of human tide.

Where I'm From

I am from the HMS *Strathaird*
in October '57 flooding Fremantle docks
with a thousand ten-pound Poms

father, mother and four of us from nine
to fifteen months were soon absorbed
into the Australian way of life

with its mind-bending heat
that strangled summer days
and tortured nights.

I am from the jacaranda streets
of Applecross lined with mauve
cushionings that crept up to

the primary school, classrooms
crammed with 50-odd kids in straight rows,
silenced by the teachers' ruler strike.

I am from the private school 'dropouts'
who fought the regimentation of life
with school ties and mental suits

and the caning of free thought –
skipping class until there was nothing
left for them to hold on to.

The Caning

I remember that cane
whistling down on the outstretched hand
like a sniper's bullet   suddenly there
to greet the moments of pain.

One, two before I knew
it's intention clear
as the flesh bleeds
from the crack of more.

The next time   the sound was gone
no outstretched hand or evil-eyed
Satan powering over me,
as I stood back   and said 'no'.

'Good on you!' my brother grinned
from more than forty years on,
at the time I wasn't to know
this act would be my final blow.

Leaving I was good at
words can't hold back teenage verve,
but I still remember that cane
and the power we shared.

Fast Food Wrappers

The first one south of the Swan
was Kentucky Fried, a
king neon sign standing
as a statement that
a New Age eatery had
come to town, almost
a mental barrier
to our normal lives –
tradition a constant silencer
of young desires,
like a forbidden word.

'It's Finger Lickin' Good'
suddenly became a catch cry
of childhood interaction
at school and on the
playing field – 'with 11 herbs
and spices' you knew you
were getting the best deal.

Hungry Jacks in Melville
was a new teenage adventure-
land of American burgers
and young girls waiting
for a stranger with a whopper
to take them with the fries

that jingle running wildly
through our minds: *'It takes
two hands, to han-dle a
whopper!'...*

Sounds good, but it was
never an easy play, long hair
and jeans an expected dialogue
that more times than not, came
unstuck between the jokes and
kisses and unzippings in-between.

Sacred Places

Applecross Jetty
once a hang-out for
'the boys' and their chicks
who'd dot the sand
in bright bikinied language

their huddled group
down by the water's edge
smoking, drinking
and spinning loud yarns
that travelled the full
length of the jetty

stuffing their towels
to hang down from
the jetty's catwalk
as curtains to the
dug-out room beneath

where couples would
disappear in mid-sentence
to claim the prize
of the afternoon –

no sacred stones
or religious rites,
just a passion for shared
love making, slipped
under the jetty sun.

Trapped in Language

Writing poems is like wagging
school, racing ambitions
around another corner,
uncertain of destinations
or who or what you'll meet.

Like any experiment the timing
must be sheered in-between
subjects or before school, some-
times recess or lunch would
provide the best human shield.

While our lives were pedestrian
we'd creep like second thoughts
around humpies on Wireless Hill:
'She roots like a rattler!' we'd
hear of conquests, no defeats.

Once minds revved behind
bonnets reaching over 1000ccs,
words raced ahead with
girlfriends   trapped in language
driving ambitions full-speed.

Writing poems is like wagging
school, escaping from life's
curriculum   to reflect
like a rear-vision mirror
anticipating what's already been.

Back-seat Vision

My daughter led me here
by chance   as if she
could read the text
of a long-forgotten now.

Dropping her at work
I drove past that lane where
you and I'd sneak passion's key
past night's expected hour.

As back door teenagers
at first on foot   then in my
Morris Minor sedan   we'd plan
the pick-up of skipping school

then cruise through the suburbs
as if we now held the key
to unlock adult pleasures
with hands shifting manual gears.

As I go back past your corner
the lights turn on the automatic
drive: 'Buckley Lane' it's called,
our footprints now recognised.

The truth is all in the name –
they had 'buckley's chance' of
finding us, as I kicked the
rear-vision mirror to one side.

Passengers

I remember the colour of her hair
golden as the sun's complexion
and her all-knowing gaze
upon me as my clumsy reach
undressed her like a combination,
a code to passion's door

all in order on the top bunk
in the Indian Pacific
reaching destinations
'before all were on board'.

Who would guess our paths
were to cross once more,
as if a planned rendezvous
at the Fremantle Markets,
both a decade older
and more self-absorbed

but with a hint of a smile
still glowing
in the distant sun
and the train's long pause

Man in the Boat

You'd hear about condoms,
but not in the same verse
as 'who you got on to'
or your latest girlfriend.

It seemed that this was the
next level of manhood
that we couldn't reach,
you had to look
at least sixteen
to get served at the pharmacy.

Although we'd send in the
'oldest looking' of us to get
the beer and spirits at hotels,
it wasn't cool to admit
that you weren't Errol Flynn

or you couldn't withdraw
before your body leaked its last
reminder… 'Oh, by the way,
this is also how you make kids!'

'Wham! Bam! Thank you Ma'am!'
we'd see the rise and fall of bodies
at the pictures or on TV
and hear the shrieks and groans

but nothing of the man in the boat
and how ambitions set sail
with the right manoeuvres.

FA Cup Nights
for Gary

Players line the couch, carpet
and walls, limbering up
they pass victory calls across
field   as beer flows
numbing brains, nudging backs
and elbows to floor

caught in motion with the stars
wrapped in coloured bonnets
and scarves with music
blaring: 'The greatest Rock 'n'
Roll band in the world – The
Who!' shouts Lionel a
leading goalkicker, as
stubbies fly across the room

intercepted out and
centre field. We're told
how Phil somersaulted
from couch to floor
with glass full landing up-
right without spilling,
still grinning

and how the crowd would
chorus Terry to drop his
pants: 'White Elephant!'
they'd yell, when the
other team scored

as the professor proportions
a hybrid in the mulling
bowl, passing his
creation from bong to hands

while 'Wacky'
a foundation member
leads the stand with abuse,
tearing strips off walls –
heroes lying pinned under
mates: 'the Deros'

like angels fallen
to this underworld
cry and sing in darkness
to their captives   clap-
ping stubbie on stubbie,
fist on door

as the whistle blows
and the goalkeeper leaves
the room   then returns,
unloading the reserves
for half-time.

Strumming Up the Past

for Greg

I can't sleep on this
bed of chords and lyrics
that held our times together
as a high school crowd

the notes of memory jumping
around in conversation, wit
and laughter leaves me
stranded inside, sitting

shoulder to shoulder with
60s and 70s rock songs from
the Small Faces, Kinks,
Beatles and Rolling Stones

calling from walls of your
teenage room   with mates and
girlfriends chorusing as your
guitar and voice took centre stage.

'50 years since we were in
Grade 1 together' a friend Jo
posted on Facebook   and now
we share this past as a meal

at Mal and Mara's place,
each year updating the lyrics
of our lives to pass around
tables before the night's

rhythm thrusts you behind guitar
as Craig and others gather,
blending our minds and voices
from memory's long-playing arm.

Neighbourhood

Neighbourhood was something that
grew out of you as a child,
passages for adventure on foot

became the loud engine roars
of teenage madness, subdued
by time and responsibility

as couples race their fortunes
hard against interest rates
and children break through

the family budget like 'one-
offs' that keep returning,
as grandparents remind you,

'You only live once…
and you're a
long time dead!'

A neighbourhood
is a pot
slowly boiling.

The Shape of Love

The Shape of Love

for my mother

I've tried to reduce your life to a poem
and failed many times before
your adventures as a rollercoaster of escapes
that flung you from childhood
in London's East End
to West Australian shores
as mother of four, grandmother
of fourteen then great-grandmother of
fifteen, before finally bringing
your journey to rest   here at ninety-four.

As second eldest in a family of six
you had to prove your mettle against
the armour of superiority given to boys,
winning a scholarship to an exclusive
girls school at age eleven where your
determined spirit elevated both confidence
and achievements, before the callings
of your mother's illness in pregnancy
and postnatal depression
pulled your eagerness unwillingly
back home at fourteen
to look after your new baby brother
and transform as housemaid to all.

Sixteen and your teenage yearnings
desired an independence not blinkered
by necessity's regime, passing tests
to become a telephonist at the
local exchange, then promoted to a senior
and transferred to the trunk exchange
at Faraday House across the road from
St Pauls at the outbreak of war –
you worked eight-hour shifts
connecting essential lines from the North
Block and straddled London's crumbling
city like an athlete during air raids,
collecting shrapnel that were
'near misses' as a trophy wall.

At eighteen a friend 'volunteered you'
into the Voluntary Fire Service – on
the Yellow Alert you would
abandon your switchboards as
phantom warriors charging to your
posts, yours on the roof or eighth floor,
as searchlights stitched the night sky together
and Spitfires outpaced Messerschmitts,
while doodlebugs or 'buzz bombs'
thundered the skies with a throbbing
drone, until their engine cut out
and they would glide   silently
as assassins to innocent lives below.

No, I can't fit all of you into this poem,
you were a master of escape
always breaking out of your life
then shaping it to give

and even now
as you lay motionless before us
with eyes closed
I sense your spirit   searching
for that open door.

The Real You

Your face showed that expression,
a typical stare forwards
as if weighing the evidence
was your barrier to the world

a defiance to all that tried to take
control of your attitudes – your
self-righteousness, wanting to be left
unchanged by all that went before.

Lying here now
with no words to explain
this sudden pause, memories
leap in front, behind

and shape the real you that
held the family together,
your devotion to your children
that stretched the decades

to grandchildren, then great-
grandchildren spreading your
love as a blanket of support
and interest in their daily lives

never missing a birthday, or
assembly item, band performance,
hockey game or award presentation
at school, just always there

was your real gift
to us all.

A Last Song

And while you were lying there
propped up in your
hospital bed   as if for a
matinee performance   it must
have been a sudden memory
or something one of us said
that brought it rushing
to your lips:

'Where did you get that hat?'
you were mouthing the
words I knew so well
from my uni days musical
'Victoriana', a song from
the 1930s inside your childhood,
infiltrating your growing years.

I remember how we'd practice
the song – Dad on piano
and you joining in
from the kitchen or suddenly
beside us – turning back
the clock, reliving those
East End of London times.

Chris and I performed in the
theatre group at Murdoch
Uni, then as part of a busload
of travelling entertainers skipping
down to country towns like
wandering minstrels to
Kojonup, to as far as Albany,
joining locals in community
halls and reeling in old timers'
friendship, singing and applause.

And while you were quietly
mouthing those words,
I wish I'd grabbed that
moment and joined you
like so many times
for one last chorus   before
that impenetrable dawn.

Deceased

in memory of my mother

She's not here
and I keep thinking
I'll ring

or visit her
before the days turn
into themselves

then suddenly picture her
doing whatever has
to be done

around here
or there   as some
existential other place

that lives
beyond seeing,
where everything has

its own sense
of meaning,
leaving us

stuck in words
that run
the full length of grief.

Rasa

Like a deluded punter
who doesn't want to miss
the promise of the next race,
I turn up at the poetry group
the day after my mother's death.

I thought I'd be all right, able
to fluke my way through
the verbal crossword of
greetings and take my place
without exposing the inner me.

Perhaps unusually quiet,
content to be just a working
part of the writing group
wheel, with no uneven
ground jarring our roll

until Shane explained the nine
Rasas are energies that define
our emotions affecting body
and mind – from erotic
through to marvellous

then the last one being
'tranquil' sent me
wallowing in the depths
of my mother's last day
and freewheeling downhill.

So Many Words

Of course you'll never
see these poems,
the words as a tribute
after you'd gone

and yet you were
always the main one
who showed interest,
wanting to keep

a copy in your file
of that part of me
you couldn't reach out to
but held with pride.

Perhaps nine or ten poems
now, so many words
to cover your lifetime roles
helping others on their paths

and tomorrow we remember
three years since you left us,
just nine days before
our daughter's wedding –

the youngest granddaughter,
your words walking her down
the aisle, 'I hope you have a
long and happy life together'

but of course, you'll
never see these poems,
the words I wish you
had heard before.

Penguin Boys

They were just like other kids
thirteen and on the cuffs
of manhood at Raines Foundation
School in London, now torn
away from their families as a
missing page in a family
manuscript – it was the first
of September 1939,
Britain's first civilian war.

'Operation Pied Piper' they
called it – three million people,
mostly schoolchildren
lined up and marched to the
train station as an infantry
of learners, labelled like
'outgoing goods', to be relocated
in the safety of 'certain' country
areas, or zones, with a hundred
thousand teachers as guardians.

My father was sent to Camberley
in Surrey with his school and
billeted with families who were
'paid a pittance' he later said, but
saw it as their 'war effort' while
students relied on BBC radio shows
like *The Radio Times* that
played classical music to ease
their adopted lives.

Charles, or 'Chuck' or 'Charlie'
and his friends Heine and 'Minky'
spoke the same language, mostly
music, literature and politics
and bought books mainly,
as '78 records were too heavy –
Penguin paperbacks for sixpence,
9d or 1 and 6 brought classical works
by Aldous Huxley, Dickens and
H.G. Wells within their reach.

They talked and talked and talked
and talked about the best bits
in their books – Penguins were
responsible for educating a whole
generation of schoolkids – on their bikes
they haunted bookshops, railway
stations or tobacconists – 'everywhere
you could find a few Penguins'.

They rode these years together
as mates, determined to keep
their time of exile and
isolation as a necessary thing,
'You just became used to it,
it was the way to live…and
reading books was something
everyone did,' my father claimed.

From childhood I watched him
reading those orange paperbacks –
leaning back, as if holding on to
the pages of his life – by the likes of
Somerset Maugham, Evelyn Waugh
and Bernard Shaw   that now sit side
by side in my bookcase   just waiting
for the Penguin boys once more.

Knitting Bones

'He was always good with bones'
my mother would say, her
mind reaching back across
continents past seventy years
to London's Blitz, watching
Spitfires chase Messerschmitts
as a hail of bright flashes
piercing the night sky.

They were stationed in Hanover
at the end of the war, my father
working under Colonel
Smythe – absorbing his teachings
as a sponge seeking all –
who recommended him as the
orthopaedic surgeon in the
British Military Hospital in Rinteln.

There was no real orthopaedics
involved, my father said, mainly
fractures/trauma – limbs in
slings or splints and plaster and
with plates and screws –
human 'carpentry' to fix
all the working pieces,
get the whole back to before.

Doctors don't heal fractures,
nature does, he claimed,
though it is often long-winded
as troops' hours in the trenches,
you can't accelerate natural
healing by 'putting your foot
down' – just create the conditions
for the best result to occur.

Some fractures do badly and
people don't fully recover –
but they expect perfection,
as if intervention is a guarantee
he explained – though working
with young, fit soldiers he found
rewarding, their bones knitting
together like units in the field.

12-bar Bones

This box of bones
inhabited my childhood,
lived inside our growing
years as part of the
family, four children
in a 4/4 time signature –
four kids to every bar.

As unexpected guests
these bones would
suddenly appear after
dark as a Hitchcock
thriller – on the kitchen
table, coffee table
or on the lounge floor

and lying scattered
as memory on the
doctor's music room
table, bones reverberating
through the Beatles, Rolling
Stones, Cream, Led Zeppelin
to Pink Floyd tunes –

60s & 70s rock anthems
that helped shape our
world – the 12-bar blues
a pulsating heartbeat
inside the bones of years.

Skeleton

I laid it out as a jigsaw
on his dining room floor,
piece by missing piece
like a cryptic message
creating shape

my father directing
pieces by name and place
as a doctor with his
anatomy students tidying
loose ends of investigation.

I look at it soaking
in the afternoon
sunlight – bones once
strewn across the growing
rooms from childhood

now a human form: 'The
first time it's been together
in 50 years' he says with
reverence – someone once
loved, now lays here alone.

'The skull is the most
emotional part' – a framework that houses the
ability to see, hear, talk,
and think   admitting

he never looks at the skull
without seeing it
covered in flesh
and wondering what kind
of person lived here.

Closing Time
for my father

I was his last paying patient
to end a fifty-six-year career,
to 'go out' with family
seemed the right thing   like a
family farewell, a send-off
that just happened to be on
June 30th to 'sweep up' accounts
for the financial year.

He escorted me to the door
as a barman at closing time,
then turned on second thoughts
saying he'd be a while
to collect his things   as I
waited in the car, wondering
what thoughts or objects
the sharp eye of memory
would suddenly hoard.

A National Health scheme refugee
he left Tilbury docks with wife
and children for Western
Australian shores in September
1957 – a time of a great 'out-flux'
of doctors he'd say, when pay
and professional satisfaction
were well below the waterline.

English doctors were paid a set
government fee – the all-free
'capitation method' assigned
patients to a doctor with a ration-
book mentality, that squeezed
patients like sheep down
narrow doorways, where
doctors were paid just
'so much per head'.

'Australian patients expected a
lot more for their money' he
maintained, 'or else they
went elsewhere!' as doctors
talked and explained in greater
detail – patient satisfaction
being the vital key to a
successful general practice door.

He started the Risely Street
practice in Applecross in the
early '60s with his partners and
saw patient numbers overtake
their lives, employing three doctors
before leaving with the sun
to work north of the river,
until a practice in the south
lured him back home.

And even now at 87 years
there's no escaping memory's
hold, as he takes our mother to
the orthopaedic surgeon who
recalls 'I heard you were
something of a legend!
…you might have been
my family doctor.'

In the rear-vision mirror
I watched him walk towards
me, preoccupied
but content with the years
placed neatly inside his
medical bag   now heaved onto
the back seat. 'Have you got
everything?' I asked
and he smiled 'yeah'.

Third Generation

Standing behind
at the piano
as a younger shadow

leaning over his shoulder
as if infiltrating
the brace of a jazz era

his fingers re-live
the irreverence of Fats Waller
at Harlem nightclubs

or 'rent parties' as we lead
chorus line: 'My very good
friend, the milkman says…'

stride pianos left hand
loose as a bohemian picking
out rolling notes and chords

that lead into 'The Joint Is
Jumping'   minds mimicking
the screech of police sirens

and burlesque asides provoking
morality's laws: '*Don't give
your right name, no no no!*'

I turn to my son 'I never
got to see my dad doing
something with his' who smiles

the bridge of generations
and picks up his trumpet,
he knows this one by heart.

Changing Speed

Going through a pile of unfinished poems
I came across a zip-top plastic bag
of locks of your hair

as if a hidden jewel of memory –
your last haircut from Carey
at our place   the locks lying in

shades of grey, but untamed
as a work of art, not wanting
to be held down to any set form

and so too, the tunes at your funeral
led us on a dance through
your life and mind:

'The Girl from Ipanema' bossa nova
by Antonio Jobim to 'Your Song' pop/rock
by Elton John, jumping back classical
to 'Claire de Lune' by Debussy

then quickstep the years to 'Us and Them'
jazz infused rock by Pink Floyd,
before leaning back to '60s rock 'n' roll
with 'Ruby Tuesday' by the Rolling Stones…

and yet there was one song missing
that few would know – 'My Very
Good Friend the Milkman'

by Fats Waller – a jazz song you said, in
your last days, 'followed you around'
from school, to London University

Medical School and finally to
your family lounge room in Australia
where Greg and I would dig out the 78s

change the record speed and sing along,
like you, embracing style and cheek
that counted back the years…

Missing Pieces

in memory of my father

(i)

They could be described
as musical pieces, those
things that you crafted
across the years:

the rose garden that
waltzed your weekends,
captivating the neighbours
and colouring the streetscape

the music room that sang
out in disparate voices
from folk, pop, rock and
jazz to classical tunes

and your piano
that once rolled from
the cheek of Fats Waller
to the roar of Beethoven

from Debussy's melodies
to Cat Stevens's acoustic dance
now lie silent, in anticipation
just waiting on your cue.

(ii)

Digging, you were always digging
and pushing wheelbarrows
of fresh earth towards
another destination

not far, maybe from back
to front yard, but
taking with you
a history of becoming

which reinvented itself
with every shovelful,
mixing soil with sacks
of mystery ingredients

like a magician, transplanting
your love of roses into
everyone's vision – up the road,
they all knew you'd been digging.

(iii)

And after dinner the ivory keys
lay waiting patiently for your
choice of favourite melodies – mainly
classical and old movie love themes

but I can't forget our duos on
Cat Stevens and other pop/rock
songs – your playing capturing the
essence   with me strumming guitar.

It's over a year since you played
your last Debussy tune   and your
final death certificate arrived
as a LP record just today:

'Death by living a long life'
it seemed to say – at 92, more than
50 as the community and family
doctor, playing other sides of you.

The Wave

There's many words in a wave –
the hand an articulator
of things not said

from greetings to farewell
the hand is a beacon
that reflects/directs feelings

of welcoming arms to
departure's last gaze, messages
signalled and meanings made.

For many years, our parents
have been waving us goodbye,
parts of their lives

driven away, casting a
network of regroupings
from the droppings off and retrievals

of grandchildren more than three decades long,
to family gatherings
bridging those islands of age.

There's many words in a wave –
the hand an articulator,
the last say.

Parents and Poems

My mother was always eager
to see my latest poems
I'd photocopy from journals
as if already stamped
with some kind of approval,
but I'd stand waiting
interested in her reply.

Some easy to pass over
that didn't venture outside
the straight blue lines,
while others sprinkled with
four-letter words, or sex
or its innuendo, creased
the margins between us

stilting conversation, some-
times left till another day,
'Did you like the poems?'
'Oh, yes,' came the answer
no elaborations expected
as the day's affairs shaded
any awkward glances.

My father was more
widely led   and perhaps
easily confined
within lust's eager hide,
even at 92, the long fingers
of memory placed him
at the point of total recall.

Applecross Jetty Bed

Chris and I came down early
wanting to absorb the breeze
of childhood memory
and the freedom we felt
roaming this shoreline
from early morn to the
reddened shadows of sun.

Graham was next, carrying
the two containers of ashes,
one in each hand steadying
his stride through the sand,
while we carried the four
smaller buckets, ready
to spread our history.

'Do you remember coming
down here with Mum and Dad?'
Jane asked, her memory longer
than her youngest brother –
No, but I can see the family
sat down on the picnic rug
diving in for sandwiches
and cordial before racing
to the Swan River's calling.

I decided each bucket should
have half mum and half
dad, like a cocktail of love
with mum first and dad on
top, making me grin inside
the morning light.

Mum would have been happy
that we all had equal shares
and while two of us cast ours
from the river's shoreline,
with the Easterly calling
for them to swim out deeper

the other two dug their ashes
in higher up the jetty sand,
one feeding them to the roots
of a bush, which would have
pleased dad, having spent
half his life in the garden –

digging out and enriching
soil for his roses, then
pruning back the years for
future family growth.

Recipe of Love

Recipe of Love

for Tracy

At first just two teachers
thrown together side by side
in classrooms that
shared a concertina wall
as if a layer that peeled back
like a protective skin

allowing each other to mix
the common points of contact
from Murdoch study days
where we were two of only
forty lives   to the music and tender
moments of flute and guitar.

But it was after sax lessons
that first lured me to your door
on a late night drive, straddling
the Swan River from south
to north, pursuing love
in its awkward moments

carrying with me the potion of
Kate Bush backing and massage
as leading lines of conversation
to break through unchartered
roads of togetherness, filled
with directions yet to come.

Now thirty years in the making
our love is a lifelong journey
with happy family turnings
in-between stretches in overdrive,
the recipe of love keeping hearts
still yearning   side by side

Gone

That sense of wonder,
surprise   travels through
childhood as a train
leading them from one
station to the next,
refuelling their day.

I remember my son
in his high chair or on
the lounge-room floor when
things went missing
we'd ask him where?
to which he'd look around
as a concerned porter
then hold up his hands
to the world: 'gone?'

Now both he and his sister
have caught the adult express
and left us here
to timetable their arrivals
and departures   with
or without luggage
and with complimentary meals.

Gone, that sense of wonder,
just visiting now   as we
walk down the empty
hallway, hear the horn blow
and gently close the
carriage door.

Eros

'Eros the melter of limbs (now again) stirs me –
Sweetbitter unmanageable creature who steals in'
– Sappho

Eros, the god of love
no wonder you're the son of Chaos,
as it leaves all of us
in somewhat disarray, capable
of complete transformation
and longings which
trace a hidden part of us
we don't yet fully know.

And later your guise as
the son of sexual love –
Aphrodite's no less,
an Errol Flynn makeover
that leaves the rest of us
limp with uncertainty

passion and fertility
oozes from your presence
within, within.

argument of seduction

well we might as well I said
almost as a throwaway suggestion

that dragged this need between us
to the forefront of our being

alone amongst the pile of
jobs that like magic keep appearing

in your speech the words all
crash together with my

thoughts all stuck wherever
there's no reason for us not to

fractures romance that we've got to
for the reason left unsaid

Love That Can't Be Tamed

Our love has travelled across
the top of the New World
where time has raced us forward
with this gift that can't be tamed

and while skiing the welcoming lips
of Lake Louise for ten days,
we learn there is a warning tucked inside
even the most alluring trails

until our hearts parallel into this day
that traces St Valentine from 496,
then celebrated as 'this day of romance'
from the fourteenth century by Chaucer:
'…*when every bird cometh there*
to choose his mate…'

to Shakespeare's words that fanned
the flames of lovers' hearts:
'*Shall I compare thee to a summer's day?*
Thou art more lovely and more temperate
…thy eternal summer shall not fade'

and yet here, in this world of climate change
our love has no season, but thrives
within our daily hearts and family,
as a gift that can't be tamed.

Symmetry

The love is in her smile
from the purse of lips
now open wide
to her neckline that drops
away like a sheer cliff
of expectation to
shoulders bronzed by
the starlight in her eyes
shimmering as a light veil
that lifts rounded breasts
with protruding eyes
to hips that surge
further down the road
towards perfect symmetry.

AFL Dogs Grand Final

Leaving wasn't easy.
A piece of my heart will stay
with her all our days.

Once back from the Game
trivialities of life
hound my every move.

If it's not weeding
it's vacuuming. My resolve:
Every dog has his day.

The Gift of Love

My love for you was sure
from our first week together,
as if time had planned
your day of arrival
as a birth into my life
nurturing friendship,
love and contentment,
knowing we would never part.

Our love grew from that
first touch in conversation,
a verbal beat in the
melody of connection
that turned our lives toward
each other, reaching out to
fine-tune feelings from
notes of common ground.

As you sleep, I peel
back time's vastness to gaze
upon the thrill of our
unfolding years, where
the lips of desire have kept
their sense of rhythm
for two hearts beating
with the gift of love.

Doorways of Love

Sitting here, the past swings back
around me, like an open doorway
that traces our beginnings

from the slender words
of greeting to the strength
and commitment of love

in just a week, our minds had
moved in together and grabbed
the laughter and joy from each other

in friendship, in respect and lust
that sang out in Irish melodies
and the pints at Clancy's

racing through to our children
Jonathan and Jaime whose lives
became our guiding sights

with the families on both sides
amassing siblings and cousins
that squeezed in family gatherings

until the years have grown
beyond us and our adult children
visit with stories and future plans

and the past, once the future
skips with our lives
through these doorways of love.

Dark Side of the Moons

My wife and I had talked it
through, as if another shared
deal, it was usually time that
sliced our lives – what's best
for the kids, this time taking
a backseat to love's certainties.

Even as I shave my neck
in morning's uncertain light
my eyes are hypnotised by
the hand's flippant strokes, till
I'm parking my car, manoeuvring
gently as an incision.

On entering I'm told 'They're
waiting for you'…stage lights
dim with excited audience chatter,
waves of nostalgia rising   then
like second thoughts, falling away
as the bedside curtain opens.

The loquacious orderly stole me,
our banter carrying me down
the corridors – how the last guy
was a frozen ball of nerves, adding
'the worst part is the anaesthetic'
as we enter the theatre doors.

She was right, the pulsing shot
burned through skin, pushing
my mind up each side of the
groin: 'I can't stand needles!'
I called out, tensing and rising
then relaxing back like after sex.

'You've done a good job shaving'
the doctor grinned at the hairless
moons, 'Yeah, I know how women
must feel shaving their bikini line!'
I laughed as the scalpel opened an
intensive interplay of hands and tools.

It was a couple of cautious days
before the after-effects showed:
'Now it's your turn to bruise!' my
wife laughed, remembering her
first birth, as I looked down
over two dark purple moons.

Love From Scott's View

Like Sir Walter Scott,
it's here my love pauses
as if on a journey
to the heart of you.

We have come as travellers
to the Scottish Borders,
our eyes reaching to the peaks
of Eildon Hills in the west,
the rolling farmlands to the south

and below us, the lush woodland
on the cliffs of the River Tweed
that 'twists and turns' as if
forever seeking the poet's words.

Suddenly transported
to the eighteenth century
by love's yearning

it's here I would halt my
carriage and undress visions
of us running free
between oak and the yellow sea
of gorse flowers

before lying breathless
in our nakedness, where love
and togetherness are absorbed
in the twists and turns
of our bodies' words.

Like Sir Walter Scott,
it's here my love pauses
as if on a journey
to the heart of you.

Where I Found Love

I listen to the lilt in your voice
singing back traditional Irish songs
that carry me carefully
like a handful of pints   past the
jug of years   to those tender moments
when my love found you.

'Whisky In a Jar', 'The Green Fields
of France' & 'Sweet Sixteen'
reverberating with the years
when you and your sisters followed
the Colonials at Clancy's Tavern
and kept the music's voice within.

And now, like the fortunes of love
that bring both tenderness & longing
I hear your singing, the lilt that
still holds me inside those tunes
where I found love
was waiting for me and you.

Love Into Words

Surrounded by places
that support/absorb love,
like a dream this could be
anywhere   and you asleep so near.

The hotel room stretches
our love to the vastness
of the Hurst Castle in San Simeon,
to the peace – a jewel we found –
on Fisherman's Harbour in Monterey

feeding imagination with clam chowder
and a South American pipe band
whose notes dance in love's melodies
as the monstrous seagulls' mating
squawks capture the sky

and otters' squeals cut the waters
surface in their hunt for love,
to the busker in San Francisco
painted gold, holding life's
heart motionless in Union Square

while cablecars pull love
into focus up impossible heights…
where we dine on each other
over the chorus of city lights.

From the Cottesloe Hotel

for Tracy

Overlooking a pearl-white beach,
Norfolk Island Pine
and ocean of aqua-dipped blue

while the band downstairs
rocks time's page, thrashing out
the sixties as a remedy to now.

Tracy and I are sinking
Stella Artois with the rays
of disappearing sun

as the rolling surf reaches us
with its strength and rhythm
and rises up and rides

the tips and curls of light
from 'The Summer of Love'
on that '60s beat.

Love in Lockdown
for Tracy

Coffee lags behind
the flavour of your smile
at once enticing us
to sip the sweetness of the day

with magpies carolling winter's song,
their cries becoming almost human wails
as they quickstep their way towards
the waiting hands of their caregivers

and I return to your welcoming smile,
the blankets of memory
wrapped around, to hold us
fast in lockdown's uncertain hands.

The Music of Love

Love doesn't always
fit into words

has more to say
than words can carry

like a tune that reaches
hearts from melody alone

words, like expectation
sometimes get in the way

yet a touch, a smile
all the things we do

become our notes
in the music of love.

The Last to Go

She had closed her eyes
as if weary with her
hundred and one years,
a silent farewell
to the family gathered
in grief and love

she, surrounded
by the warmth of memories
from Albany to her
North Fremantle home
that watched each of her
three children and
extended family grow.

I leaned over to my wife
and whispered 'I think
we should leave'…and
one of her grandmother's
eyes opened quickly
as a shutter of daggers
that pierced my words,
pinning me back, as if
I was impatient to exit.

Later I was told
that hearing is the last
sense to go.

Rottnest Ghost

Rottnest Ghost

Setting out at dusk
at least fifty nameless souls
met outside the museum,
at first like a pub – the brawl
of voices all waiting
for who we didn't know.

'The art of storytelling is lost
nowadays' our host tossed
amongst us, lowering his head
drawing us within his range,
as we stood, dark as shadows that
chilled tales of the unexplained.

Then we sat together as strangers
in the darkness that bound us,
a smorgasbord of races
from children to the old
our minds tense in anticipation
urging secrets out of what is known.

Led as prisoners in the shackles
of night, along thin lines of light
and memory to Thomsons Bay,
we find the narrow limestone prison
where convicts were stored as standing
baggage, lashed by wave and sand.

He tells of the Aboriginal prisoner
whose life was beaten to his grave,
but as a 'flame in the night sky'
vowed revenge – haunting convicts
and pushing lighthouse keepers to
their end, 'before his rage was spent'.

Our ranks have now closed, as
we leave the cemetery, where
thirteen lives are buried, but only
seven named, the stark breeze
tearing through windcheaters,
awakening the ghost within us all.

The Hunger Beneath

Nets lay as ghosts
fishing below the waves,
seizing up to three times
the capacity of
what the ocean can sustain

then wrap themselves
like outdated policies around
reefs and marine mammals –
seals, whales and dolphins –
as serial killers for decades.

Death comes to others as an elixir
of oil and liquid spills
from fishing vessels,
until our final net is thrown
and captures a hungry world.

Surfcatting on the Swan

Unloading the trailer at Crawley Bay
we wait for the sea breeze – the bane
of surfers looking for a good ride –
quickly rigging main sail with
rudder pins, stays and sheets
pulled hard on into the race
between nature and life man-made.

Feeling the breeze as traffic lights
trying to direct our gain – algal
blooms flash blue-green below
as growth from nutrients
seeps through our years,
land imbued with fertilisers

and generations of sprays
driving governments' open-
hand policies, leak the truth
to a new decade – the Fremantle
doctor's steady knife cuts
deep as two hulls slicing
waves of consciousness.

Freedom races through eyes
and smiles as we sheer past
the Majestic Hotel and a
childhood of other haunts
now gone – our history
reclaimed and sold off
as time rushes the
other way:

on the wind, beating into it,
dead run, jiving, going
about, shy run – my head
reels with these terms as
anglers cast wary lines

and I feel the future cold
biting at memory's
joints: 'man against
the elements' –the
challenge in
our lives.

Flight of Love

The long, low howling
rode the breeze through our
kitchen window, inviting
us as guests to morning
and evening song – doves
perched precariously
as tightrope walkers on
a wooden veranda beam.

Almost within reach, she is
the expectant mother,
motor purring to the sky's
vastness, eyeing us off
with disdain from her shallow
weathered nest, proclaiming
rights of tenure – having
staked out her territory first.

Our cats watched, suddenly
becoming frozen cameo
and sleek grey toys,
summing up their chances
as the doves are tuned
to a distant call…one
good leap perhaps, no
pole's too steep and smooth,
teasing access, a karma
twist placing them as
audience in desire's game.

The weeks brought urgent
voices and bustling verve,
stressing sparse surrounds,
as the dutiful mother
becomes hunter, feeder,
protector nurturing
nature's call, guiding their
spirits with skill and
discipline in preparation
for that one day.

The Saturday sleep-in
wasn't planned, but on
hearing our children's
plethora of ideas and games
drum up the hall, we lapsed
into time's protection
as our cats ravaged the
baby doves' unsteadiness,
hurling feathers as a
solemn vestige on the lawn.

As our children's hearts
weep for what this day could
have been, the parents
return, following love's
scent to their children's
shallow graves below.

The long, low howling
rode the breeze through our
kitchen window, inviting
us as guests to morning
and evening song.

Not to Know

Today wasn't a normal day
to find Zoe out after dusk
and even when called
for her to hiss and arch away
as a lioness defending her lair.

Not feeling like the chase and stealth
needed to manoeuvre her inside,
I let her go with the shadows
not realising in half an hour this
Burmese child would return no more.

Looking at you, frozen on bitumen
as if time had momentarily stilled,
you seem larger, with fur shock-
teased, your gaze unchanging
looking further on, past now.

You were a wanderer, just like
the Oriental Siamese, known by
strangers blocks away and the big
black and white cat wandering curiously
past the back glass laundry door.

Telling our children was hardest:
Jaime and her spontaneous waterfall
of tears   and Jonathan, the older
holding his back, shouting, 'She wasn't
even a year old!' his tears wouldn't let go.

In some ways I'm prepared for
your death, having rehearsed
the loss when you once disappeared,
'not knowing' imbuing a stronger hope
that suddenly burst through the door.

As I look at you, snug in your bed
by the camellias, I turn and curl your
body evenly with the shovel, as if
moulding a pot in clay, echoing your
despair: 'I came running when you called…'

And I still hear you, scratching, climbing
on the back flywire, absorb your
rich purring memory in early dawn,
watching the black and white cat wander
hopefully, past the glass laundry door.

Intruders

I'd seen a black form
low to the ground as a rat
streak like lightning
across our back garden bed

but this morning, its movements
slowed as the breeze, while this
brown animal forages amongst
undergrowth like a quokka.

It lifts its head, as if wanting
the recognition of name – yes, a
southern brown bandicoot or
'Quenda' visits in daylight

from its Murdoch Hospital
bush home – a small mammal
seeking earthworms and other
invertebrates, even turning its snout

to fungi and subterranean plant
material like other omnivores,
digging up this forest treasure
with powerful forearms and claws

as if to keep the species 'hanging on'
in Perth, while their cousins in
crowded eastern cities have gone.
Solitary creatures, they build

dome-shaped nests in dense
vegetation as we watch in silence
through our window as intruders,
stealing in on this natural world.

Being Frank

One can only live so
long with a woman
is all he said,
eyes curling in corners
like a protective
grin, wishing
you well
away from him.

I think you were silly
asking her to go
I leaned closer drinking
this German beer,
I don't think it was
his face
expressionless
and wary   she has
her beliefs
and I have mine.

Perhaps silly is the
wrong word
she just seemed
so nice   she
is his dark eyes
slid in quick
but I'm not in the
marriage market
or anything.

Feeling like I'd
crashed a party
I sat back
and watched him talk
his eyes alert
but as if
it didn't matter
who was there.

He doesn't need
anyone   an ex-girlfriend
said   that's just Frank.

Haibun

for Chris R.

As a friend and as fathers,
I can only weep with your family over this turn of flight,
your new start pursuing the robot eye of medical imaging,
stretched the limits of your journey of studentship
against the steady pulse of full-time teaching of your wife.

Your gift and love of flying aircraft returned little in the
family coffers, but remained your personal dream, inside
the emptiness of night.

Those car exhaust fumes
trapped inside
freed you.

Fremantle: in Spirit and Voice

for Liana Joy Christensen

We meet first on the lawn as
strangers outside the Round House
at Arthur Head   our bodies
shimmering in the reddened glows
of setting sun across the bay
while children free their
spirits in the shallows of
water and beach below.

We are led as prisoners
of time to our first destination,
down stairs to the Whaler's
Tunnel that cuts through the
limestone cliffs of Arthur Head
to High Street as the sun falls sharply
into the ocean's patient reach.

Suddenly a hundred strong,
crammed in with the years
inside this blackened archway
we listen to the 'whispering walls'
tell of Aboriginal incarceration
in the Round House and of others
exiled to Rottnest's 'Aboriginal
Prison' – their tortured cries from
the Quod speaking out in Liana's
poetry, echoing mysteriously on.

As we stand transfixed by the
savage text of our history, a
voice shoots out from the darkness
singing 'Kiss the Children for Me
Mary' with another voice
in harmony, as if to soothe
the fare of these colonial days,
before rousing the voices of all:

'Come all you screw warders and jailers
Remember Perth Regatta Day,
Take care of the rest of your Fe-ni-ans
Or the Yankees will steal them away…'

the tunnel bellowed in chorus,
as the lyrics from 'The Catalpa'
became much more, stringing
a line tightly between us
as laden vessels tied to
this place and conviction.

Preston Point

I start my journey as a poem
suddenly thrown onto the page
on a track by the Left Bank Hotel
East Fremantle foreshore

the sky as my opponent
threatening rain as I climb up
the cut limestone steps
behind the brawl of voices

as if I'm entering a hidden
land   shielded in part
by its proximity to now:
Tuart, Peppermint, Fremantle

Mallee, Rottnest Island Pine,
Sheoak and other inhabitants
have adapted to life here
drinking discreetly between

high alkaline rock and sand.
Walking east along the limestone
ridge formed by nature's
sculpturing, from compaction

and leaching of marine deposits
beneath the dunes that have
disappeared with time's
accomplices of wind and rain

the Swan River's meanderings
have carved out a rock face
that stares back with
beauty's rage.

A waterfall coaxes my
steps, through green and
variegated leaves, down
a series of levels it plays

then gushes forth to the
river shore at Preston Point:
'Niergarup' – Noongar for
'the place where pelicans meet' –
a 'bush supermarket' before
the arrival of the white spirits
who fenced off their land,
restricting their blood flow

as land grants swooped as crows
down to the Canning and Swan
River shores claiming sacred
sites and traditional hunting grounds

'Noongar territory' and people
with different cultures and
beliefs now herded as cattle,
suddenly thrown into one.

And do we feel Yagan's pain
when trust and friendship
were betrayed? It was here
at Preston Point that he

vowed revenge for his brother's
death   Yagan's head was to
carry a price tag of 30 pounds –
'for a working man, a year's wage'.

I started my poem as a journey
thrown onto a dirt track
beneath the dunes   that
ended at a ferry crossing.

Porongorups to Bluff Knoll

From Karri Chalets
to the foot of Nancy's Peak,
the sun rises sharply
with rocks and trees
where white arrows remind
us we're not the first.

We puff our way via
Devil's Slide and
Hollywood Peak on
igneous & metamorphic
rock – a thousand hardened
eyes watching our gaits
as bookmakers, taking
bets on who will reach.

On top of the Porongorups
rocks flash multicoloured
lichen – white, light-green,
orange and pink – while
twigs become lizards and
wriggling salamander and a lone
grass tree stands resolute
as a palm in this rock oasis.

The Warnsborough Walk
uncoils like a snake, as
Pee Wees flit through
the slowed breeze   and we
hear the sound of water
rushing as children,
playing somewhere in
this menagerie of leaves.

At Nancy's Peak the sun
whitens fallow fields, the
Stirling Ranges appear as a
mauve outline becoming
the neck, breast and
legs of a sleeping woman
as red gums rise above
enclosing our trail

as giant onlookers above
clay steps surrounded
by soil   where Tracy
and I part on weary
terms   and I straddle the
diced sedimentary rocks
in the shade of duty
and expectation.

I pass the dry ledges
of a waterfall – an absent
friend suddenly missed –
and realise this climb
can't be captured by
words' playfulness, away
from the sweat and
camaraderie of rock and tree.

Shale rock peaks
surround this Olympus,
where the wind runs swiftly
as the Gods' messenger
gently throwing flower petals
to colour this barren crown.

Windhold Day

From our ski lodge window
full-breasted eucalypts erupt
from this whitened alpine
landscape, refusing to let life be
smothered by the coat of now.

It's a 'Windhold Day' at
Falls Creek where the wayward
wind has closed all lifts, skiers
and snowboarders (suddenly)
pedestrian as precipitation's
gentle artist hand counter-
points the dark tones
of snow gums with the
bright melody of snow.

We sit in Be Food Store sharing
tapas plates, chewing over the
'What the's… and 'What if's…
as fog surrounds our conversation,
crowded on the outside glass
as eager ears wanting to help
shape the dalliance of plans.

'This day cannot be wasted' –
a resolution unsaid, but in each
mental frame, as we catch the
shuttle up to Windy Corner,
swill down large coffees
to charge our inner linings
and look hopefully up the
slope of Wombat's Ramble.

As we battle the freezing wind
that shoots up your nose as
a precise radar – even as we
reverse like the over-snow
vehicles and walk
backward up the slope –
we are pushed down
two steps to every one.

We pass a lone worker who
calls out 'you've gone a third
of the way and there's two
more to go!' so we turn around
on a unanimous decision
without words, allowing
gravity to seduce us
and lead us astray

down to the Harvey Wallbanger
Hour at the Falls Creek Hotel –
the guitarist thrashing back
the past just like a white-out
hits you head on: 'Summertime',
'Hotel California' and
'Knocking On Heaven's Door'
blasting memories through.

We ended up at Stingray
Bar where tables are packed
with huddled voices
safe from the wild wind
that wouldn't let go, now
dissecting their frozen day:
'Well, there's always glühwein!'
Tracy smiles across the room.

Back at Diana Lodge
we open the sliding glass door
to the eager appetites of
magpies and currawongs, as
the snow waits patiently below.

Norseman Moon

White cratered disc
pasted on aqua-blue,
today you appear at 30 degrees

looking hungry
before breakfast –
it must be winter on the moon.

This morning captured by fluted
voices chasing each other
up and around the scales

as magpies gather in tribes
in strict social order,
lining up for roll call

then swiftly retreating
in unison   as if
suddenly called from afar –

lifting their wings
and shooting off like
diagonal passes across field

cart-wheeling direction,
sheering bushes and eucalypts
with panic and fear

then disappearing
as commandos in camouflage
between leaf and tree

under this petrified form
suspended as thought,
on aqua-blue.

Looking Glass

Unfinished
bits of me   jut out
like a table corner,
just far enough
to dislodge thinking

send me hurtling
down pathways
that twist and dive
through time
with reflected ease

magnifying words,
those stark desert
nights on Norseman's
inland shore

with you   as the
tide   turning
inside me.

Raffles Hotel on Song

'The Highway to Hell'
it was called, from the '60s to
'70s, that crazy stretch of
Highway from Bon Scott's house
in North Fremantle – bodies
packed tightly as beer bottles

in EH & FJ Holdens and
panel vans, drinks passed
as a magic potion from
hand to hand with radio blaring,
to Sleat Road Applecross
they'd put their foot down

as the road dips in harmony
into a steep decline
to the Raffles crossroad
where cars loaded with
teenage voices would race
through to end their song.

A 'rock 'n' roll drinking hole'
with brawls starting on the
dance floor, then thrown out
to the carpark where police paddy
wagons and truncheons out in force
steered the end of night crowd.

We knew this as the old way
and yet, even last year,
another punch-up
on the dance floor
left a young guy unconscious
fighting another round.

Snake Pit Scarborough Beach

On the concrete terraced pit
waiting as a '50s rock and roll
invasion on the beachfront,
Bill Haley and His Comets
blasted teenage senses with
'Rock Around the Clock'
from a jukebox that wouldn't give up.

Dancing till the midnight toll
the Snake Pit writhed with the
songs of Eddie Cochran, Gene
Vincent and Bo Diddley hammering out
'I'm a Man' in twelve- bar blues.

The main fights were over
girls, as blokes competed in duels
on the dance floor, or in conversations,
or from lingering looks that burst
the jealousy bubble.

Bodgies dressed in stovepipe pants
with black or white T-shirts
and long, slicked-back Brylcreem hair,
to Widgies in skirts with petticoats
or tight sewn-in jeans
and short hairstyles, teased the
clean-cut news reports and their
damning verbs:

'notorious', 'blared' and 'strutted'
as hundreds to a thousand
teenagers laughed and jived
in and around the Snake Pit
and couldn't get enough.

Petrarchan Ode to Woodstock

'It's been a long time since I rock and rolled'
Led Zeppelin
thrashing through punk, new wave, before indie
gripped teenagers
minds and more, forgetting the lust and thrill
of Alvin Lee and Jimi Hendrix lead
guitar chasing
the blues away
from Vietnam – three days of love.

To the Edge of Now

in memory of Kim

More than thirty years gone
your memory still stirs
love's places   Perth,
Lancelin and Sydney as
teenage to adult playgrounds,
locked inside our tears.

Only your letters remain
filled with energy and
commitment from anti-uranium
writing, marching and
Hiroshima Day, to your
sexual politics stripping
honesty and building wimin's
self-image in discussion groups,
conferences and weekends away.

And yet your words always
regretted time's double-
edge   the one that
offered fulfilment at a self-
destructive pace   freeing
doubt and loneliness
in relationships that reached
for what you were now without.

More than thirty years gone
your sister and I swap
knowings and tales
that bring your laughter
racing back.

Regret

In the black of night
I find you

lingering in some
worn memory

that throws a hook
to the moments of now

dragging thought un-
willingly   as a prisoner

of time's journeys
towards the light of day.

Dispiriting

The streets of Perth, Northbridge
blinded by fluorescent lights flashing
and penetrating your being

and the lifeless bodies tucked up
in sleeping bags and newspapers
that line shop frontages

with remains of drink and fast food
spilling their sweetness
onto the sidewalk

as if offerings
to the insects, that will
one day inch them away.

Stumps

Three days and I retire
after a thirty-two-year innings

at last I'm out

caught behind or clean bowled?
I can't be sure.

Acknowledgements

Thank you to the editors of the following journals and anthologies for publishing some of these poems: *Going Down Swinging, Creatrix, Poetry Monash, Regime, The Mozzie, Southerly, Poetry d'Amour 2017, 2018* and *2020, Recoil 10, Rabbit, Mad About You: 40 Years of Fremantle Arts Blog, Echidna Tracks, Creatrix Anthology 2 2012–2016,* The *High Window, Windmills, Locus – OOTA Writers Anthology 2019, Brushstrokes – Ros Spencer Poetry Contest Anthology 2016–2019, Reflections and Introspections 2019 Anthology* by the Vincent Writers Group and *Creatrix Anthology 3 2017–2020.*

'Cicadas' was Commended in the 2014 Kimberley Haiku Festival of Words Corrugated Lines.

'From Bar to Spyglass' was Equal First in the 2016 Creatrix Poetry Prize.

'Recipe of Love' was Highly Commended in the 2017 Poetry d'Amour Love Poetry Competition.

'The Poem Itself' was Commended in the 2018 Creatrix Occasional Poetry Prize to mark the 40th Edition and 10th anniversary of the online journal.

'A Last Song' was Commended in the 2019 Creatrix Poetry Prize.

'Missing Pieces' won First prize in the 2019 Tom Collins National Poetry Prize.

Poems have been read as feature poet at the Perth Poetry Club,

Poetry by the Sea at Scarborough Beach, Voicebox and the Poetry Bites reader for the OOTA Poetry Group at the Fremantle Arts Centre.

Mike has been interviewed and read his poetry on Jenny Pretty's *Antipodean Experience*, Radio Fremantle 107.9 FM; *The World of Art*, Peter Jeffery OAM, 6EBA, 95.3 FM; and *Noonday Carousel*, Peter Jeffery OAM, KCR, 102.5 FM.

Thank you to Angie A. Phillips (Angie@angcreative design.co.uk) for her artistic front cover design.

Thanks

Special thanks to Peter Jeffery (and his wife Julie) who has become a close friend, poetry collaborator and 'drinking partner' at the Perth Poetry Club in the Moon Café in Northbridge. I have enjoyed working alongside him in editing some issus of Creatrix online and the *Creatrix Anthology 2*. Peter has been very encouraging and supportive of my writing over the years and he helped me select the poems for this collection.

I would like to thank the writing friends at the Moon in Northbridge and the Out of the Asylum (OOTA) Poetry Group at the Fremantle Arts Centre for their encouragement and support. Shane McCauley's fortnightly OOTA Poetry Group has been one of the highlights of poetry workshops over recent years and I thank him for his expertise, friendship and motivation.

There are too many names of writing friends to thank for their support, but I must mention Ross Jackson and Jan Napier, who have been my writing buddies at OOTA and beyond. Also Alan Padgett for his welcoming manner and friendship to new poets at the Moon, and Elio Novello as a friendly and judicious coordinating MC of the Perth Poetry Club.

As a WAPI Festival committee member, I have appreciated the way we have created the festival year in, year out, and the superb efforts of our leader Gary De Piazzi.

Last, but not least, I would like to thank my wife Tracy for her love and support of my poetry (and other peculiarities) for over thirty years.

www.ingramcontent.com/pod-product-compliance
Lightning Source LLC
Chambersburg PA
CBHW070859080526
44589CB00013B/1138